Amelia Island

Travel Guide 2025

Enjoy the Amazing Attractions with Tips on When to Visit

Bryan J. Zehner

Disclaimer: The information, contacts, websites, and costs provided in this book were accurate at the time of publication. Readers are advised to verify current details as information may have changed since publication.

Content

Introduction

Amelia Island, a barrier island located in the northeastern part of Florida, is a captivating destination known for its pristine beaches, rich history, and vibrant culture. Unlike many other tourist-heavy locations in Florida, Amelia Island offers a unique blend of tranquility and adventure, making it a perfect getaway for travelers looking to experience both relaxation and exploration. With its picturesque landscapes, well-preserved historic sites, and a welcoming community, the island provides an inviting atmosphere for visitors of all kinds. Whether you are interested in discovering local history, indulging in culinary delights, or enjoying outdoor activities, Amelia Island has something for everyone.

As the world continues to evolve, travel trends shift, and destinations like Amelia Island gain popularity for their natural beauty and cultural significance. The 2025 travel season presents an ideal time to visit, with new attractions, improved accommodations, and an array of events that highlight the best of what the island has to offer. This guide serves as a comprehensive resource for those planning to explore Amelia Island, providing essential details on what to see, where to stay, and how to make the most of your visit. Whether you are a first-time traveler or a returning visitor, this guide will ensure that your experience on Amelia Island is both memorable and fulfilling.

Welcome to Amelia Island

Amelia Island, part of the Sea Islands chain along the U.S. East Coast, is often regarded as one of Florida's best-kept secrets. Spanning just 13 miles in length and about four miles in width, this island boasts an unparalleled combination of natural beauty and historical significance. With its picturesque beaches, maritime forests, and charming downtown area, Amelia Island offers a distinct experience that sets it apart from other Florida destinations.

The island's history dates back thousands of years, with evidence of Native American habitation long before European explorers arrived. The Timucua people were among the first inhabitants, living off the land and the surrounding waters. The arrival of European explorers in the 16th century marked the beginning of a complex history that saw Amelia Island change hands multiple times. Over the centuries, the island has been under the control of eight different nations, earning it the nickname "Isle of Eight Flags." Today, this rich history is preserved in the island's architecture, museums, and cultural heritage sites.

One of the most striking features of Amelia Island is its well-preserved environment. Unlike many other Florida destinations that have experienced extensive commercial development, Amelia Island remains committed to conservation and sustainability. Fort Clinch State Park, a 1,400-acre protected area, offers visitors the chance to explore coastal dunes, salt marshes, and a historic 19th-century fort. Meanwhile, the Amelia Island Greenway provides a network of scenic trails ideal for biking and walking.

The local community plays a significant role in maintaining the island's welcoming and laid-back atmosphere. Residents take pride in their hometown, and this is evident in the island's locally-owned businesses, art galleries, and annual festivals. The hospitality of Amelia Island's people adds to its charm, making visitors feel at home from the moment they arrive. Whether you are strolling through the historic streets of Fernandina Beach or enjoying a meal at a family-owned restaurant, you will find that the warmth and friendliness of the locals enhance the overall experience.

Why Visit Amelia Island in 2025?

Amelia Island has always been a popular destination, but 2025 presents an especially compelling time to visit. Several factors make this year an ideal time to experience everything the island has to offer. From upcoming events to new accommodations and attractions, visitors in 2025 can expect an enriched travel experience.

One of the major highlights of 2025 is the expansion of cultural and recreational activities.

The annual Isle of Eight Flags Shrimp Festival, held in May, continues to be one of the most anticipated events of the year. This festival celebrates the island's shrimping industry with a weekend filled with parades, live music, local crafts, and, of course, plenty of fresh seafood. The Amelia Concours d'Elegance, one of the most prestigious classic car shows in the world, is set to return in March, attracting car enthusiasts from all over the globe.

New developments in hospitality and tourism infrastructure also make 2025 an exciting time to visit. Several hotels and resorts have undergone renovations, offering visitors more luxurious and comfortable accommodations. Boutique hotels in Fernandina Beach have introduced new amenities, ensuring that guests enjoy a blend of historic charm and modern convenience. For those seeking a more immersive experience, vacation rental options have expanded, allowing travelers to stay in beachfront cottages, historic homes, and eco-friendly lodgings.

Culinary experiences on Amelia Island continue to evolve, with new restaurants and bars adding to the island's already impressive dining scene. Seafood remains a staple, with restaurants sourcing fresh catches directly from local waters. Additionally, 2025 sees the introduction of farm-to-table dining experiences, where visitors can enjoy meals made from locally grown ingredients. The island's craft beverage scene is also thriving, with new breweries and distilleries offering tastings and tours.

Outdoor enthusiasts will find that Amelia Island remains one of the best destinations for nature-based activities. Kayaking through the island's salt marshes, paddleboarding along the coastline, and fishing in its pristine waters are just a few of the adventures available. In 2025, new guided eco-tours provide deeper insights into the island's unique ecosystems, allowing visitors to learn about local wildlife and conservation efforts. Birdwatching remains a favorite pastime, as the island is home to a diverse range of bird species, including osprey, egrets, and pelicans.

Best Time to Visit

Choosing the best time to visit Amelia Island depends on personal preferences, but each season offers a unique experience. The island enjoys a mild climate year-round, making it an appealing destination no matter the month. However, certain times of the year provide specific advantages based on weather, events, and crowd levels.

Spring is one of the most popular times to visit, with temperatures ranging from the mid-60s to the upper 70s. This season is ideal for outdoor activities, such as hiking, biking, and exploring Fort Clinch State Park. Spring also hosts some of the island's most significant events, including the Isle of Eight Flags Shrimp Festival and the Amelia Concours d'Elegance. The pleasant weather and vibrant festivities make this a prime time for travelers looking to experience the island at its liveliest.

Summer is perfect for those who enjoy beach vacations. From June through August, temperatures rise into the 80s, providing excellent conditions for swimming, sunbathing, and water sports. While summer is a peak tourist season, the island's beaches offer plenty of space to relax and unwind. Families particularly enjoy this time of year, as school vacations allow for extended stays. It is important to note that summer also brings occasional afternoon thunderstorms, a common feature of Florida's climate.

Fall offers a more relaxed atmosphere, with fewer crowds and pleasant temperatures in the 70s. This season is great for visitors who prefer a quieter experience while still enjoying outdoor activities. The autumn months also bring beautiful coastal sunsets and special seasonal events, such as food and wine festivals. The lower humidity and gentle breezes make exploring the island's historic sites and nature trails particularly enjoyable.

Winter is the least crowded time to visit, providing a peaceful retreat for those looking to escape colder climates. With temperatures in the 50s and 60s, the island remains mild compared to many other destinations. The holiday season brings festive decorations to downtown Fernandina Beach, creating a charming and cozy atmosphere. Travelers can take advantage of off-season rates on accommodations while still experiencing all the island has to offer.

Chapter 1

Getting to Amelia Island

Amelia Island, located in the northeastern corner of Florida, is a prime destination known for its pristine beaches, historic charm, and vibrant local culture. Travelers have multiple options to reach this beautiful island, whether by air, road, or public transportation. Careful planning will ensure a smooth and enjoyable journey.

Amelia Island is easily accessible by air, with Jacksonville International Airport (JAX) being the closest major airport. Located about 30 miles from the island, this airport serves numerous domestic and international flights daily. Airlines such as Delta, American Airlines, Southwest, and United offer direct and connecting flights from various locations across the United States and beyond. Upon arrival at JAX, travelers have multiple ground transportation options, including rental cars, shuttles, and ride-sharing services like Uber and Lyft. The airport shuttle service, operated by Amelia Island Transportation, offers direct transport from Jacksonville International Airport to the island, with fares typically ranging from $60 to $80 per trip. For inquiries and reservations, contact Amelia Island Transportation at (904) 753-6480 or visit their website at www.ameliaislandtransportation.com.

For those preferring private car services, several luxury and executive transportation companies operate between Jacksonville and Amelia Island. Services such as East Coast Transportation and Jax Black Car offer premium private rides with costs varying based on vehicle type and distance. East Coast Transportation can be reached at (904) 525-8600, and their website is www.ectjax.com. Jax Black Car offers premium chauffeur services with bookings available through their website at www.jaxblackcar.com or by calling (904) 372-8084.

Visitors driving to Amelia Island can access the island via Interstate 95, one of the major highways connecting Florida with the rest of the East Coast. Travelers coming from the north can take Exit 373 in Florida, which connects to State

Road A1A East, leading directly to Amelia Island. Those traveling from the south can also use Exit 373 or opt for scenic coastal routes, such as Highway 17, which offers picturesque views of marshlands and historic sites. Parking on Amelia Island is convenient, with many hotels, resorts, and public beach areas offering free or low-cost parking.

A road trip to Amelia Island allows travelers to explore several attractions along the way. For those driving from major cities such as Atlanta, the journey takes approximately five hours via I-75 South and I-10 East. From Miami, expect a drive of about six hours, taking I-95 North. For visitors coming from Orlando, the drive is around three hours using I-4 East and I-95 North. Fuel prices fluctuate, but as of early 2025, the average gas price in Florida is around $3.50 per gallon. It is recommended to check current fuel rates before embarking on a road trip.

Public transportation options on Amelia Island are limited but efficient for those who prefer not to drive. Nassau Transit provides shuttle services on the island and surrounding areas. The Amelia Island Trolley, a charming and convenient way to explore the island, operates on a fixed route with stops at popular tourist destinations, including Fernandina Beach Historic District, Fort Clinch State Park, and Main Beach Park. A one-day trolley pass costs approximately $10 per person. More information about schedules and stops can be found at www.ameliatrolley.com or by calling (904) 277-0717.

Bicycle rentals are another popular way to explore Amelia Island. Several bike rental companies offer hourly, daily, and weekly rental options. Popular providers include Amelia's Wheels, which offers a variety of bicycles, including tandem bikes and electric bikes. Rental prices start at $15 per hour, and more details can be found at www.ameliaswheels.com or by calling (904) 261-6161. Pedego Electric Bikes also provides e-bike rentals for easier navigation across the island's scenic trails, with rental costs starting at $25 per hour. Pedego can be contacted at (904) 310-6657, and their website is www.pedegoelectricbikes.com.

For visitors relying on taxis and ride-sharing services, Uber and Lyft operate on Amelia Island, providing convenient transport options for short distances. Local taxi companies such as Amelia Island Taxi and Shuttle offer reliable services with competitive rates. Amelia Island Taxi can be reached at (904) 753-8885, and more details can be found on their website at www.ameliaislandtaxi.com.

Amelia Island is also accessible by boat, with Fernandina Harbor Marina serving as the main docking point for private and commercial vessels. This full-service marina offers docking facilities, fueling stations, and boating supplies. Docking fees vary based on vessel size and duration of stay. The marina can be contacted at

(904) 310-3300, and their website is www.fernandinaharbor.com.

For visitors traveling by train, the nearest Amtrak station is in Jacksonville, approximately 30 miles from Amelia Island. From the Amtrak station, travelers can take a taxi, shuttle, or rental car to the island. Amtrak provides routes from various locations across the United States, with ticket prices varying based on departure city and class of service. For schedules and booking, visit www.amtrak.com or call (800) 872-7245.

Chapter 2

Top Attractions & Must-See Sights

Fort Clinch State Park stands as one of Amelia Island's most iconic historical landmarks. Spanning over 1,400 acres, this well-preserved 19th-century fort offers visitors the chance to step back in time and experience military history firsthand. The fort, constructed in 1847, was used during the Civil War, Spanish-American War, and even as a lookout during World War II. Guests can explore the brick fortress, walk along the cannons, and witness reenactments that bring history to life. The surrounding state park also offers nature trails, camping, and a beach with stunning views of the Cumberland Sound. The entry fee for the park is $6 per vehicle, with an additional $2.50 per person for fort access. Visitors can contact Fort Clinch State Park at (904) 277-7274, and additional information is available on their website at www.floridastateparks.org

For those interested in lighthouses, the Amelia Island Lighthouse is a must-visit. This historic beacon, built in 1838, is the oldest lighthouse in Florida still in operation. Sitting atop a bluff, it provides panoramic views of the island and the Atlantic Ocean. Though the lighthouse itself is not open for general admission, guided tours are available twice a month, allowing visitors to learn about its history and significance. The cost for a guided tour is $5 per person, and reservations are required. The Amelia Island Lighthouse can be reached at (904) 310-3350, with more details available at www.fbfl.us

Historic Downtown Fernandina Beach is the heart of Amelia Island's charm. This area is rich in Victorian-era architecture, boutique shops, and local restaurants, making it perfect for an afternoon stroll. Visitors can explore the Amelia Island Museum of History, housed in the former Nassau County jail, where exhibits highlight the island's past from Native American settlements to Spanish and British rule. The museum's admission fee is $10 for adults and $5 for children. Downtown also features local artisan markets, live music, and annual festivals that showcase the island's vibrant culture. Visitors can learn more about Historic Downtown

Fernandina Beach by calling (904) 277-0717 or visiting www.ameliaisland.com

American Beach carries significant cultural and historical value, known as a haven for African Americans during segregation. Established in the 1930s by Abraham Lincoln Lewis, Florida's first Black millionaire, American Beach was a thriving vacation destination for Black families who were not allowed to visit other segregated beaches. Today, the beach remains a symbol of resilience and history, with the A.L. Lewis Museum providing insight into its rich heritage. Visitors can enjoy the pristine coastline, take a guided tour, and learn about the role American Beach played in the Civil Rights Movement. The museum has a suggested donation of $5 for entry. Contact information for American Beach and the A.L. Lewis Museum is available at (904) 510-7036, and more details can be found at www.nps.gov/timu

The Palace Saloon holds the distinction of being Florida's oldest continuously operating bar. Established in 1903, it has served as a gathering place for sailors, locals, and visitors alike. The bar features a rich wooden interior with Tiffany-style lamps and an extensive selection of drinks, including its signature Pirates Punch. The Palace Saloon provides an authentic Old Florida atmosphere where visitors can unwind and enjoy live music. There is no entry fee, but drink prices range from $6 to $15. Visitors can contact the saloon at (904) 491-3332 or visit www.thepalacesaloon.com for additional details.

For those looking for nearby accommodations, the Omni Amelia Island Resort offers a luxurious stay with oceanfront rooms, multiple dining options, and a full-service spa. Nightly rates start at approximately $300, and reservations can be made by calling (904) 261-6161 or visiting www.omnihotels.com. Another excellent option is the Amelia Hotel at the Beach, which provides comfortable and affordable accommodations just steps from the ocean. Room rates start at around $180 per night. Guests can call (904) 206-5600 or visit www.ameliahotel.com for bookings. For a more boutique experience, the Addison on Amelia offers a charming bed-and-breakfast stay with personalized service. Room rates begin at $250 per night, and reservations can be made by calling (904) 277-1604 or visiting www.addisononamelia.com

Chapter 3

Best Beaches and Outdoor Adventures

Main Beach Park is one of the most accessible and well-maintained beaches on Amelia Island. Located at 32 N Fletcher Ave, Fernandina Beach, this park is an excellent spot for families and individuals looking to soak up the sun, play beach volleyball, or enjoy a picnic by the ocean. The park features ample parking, restrooms, and outdoor showers, ensuring convenience for visitors. There are also picnic tables and grills available for those who want to have a beachside meal. The beach is free to access, and visitors can find nearby accommodations at the Seaside

Amelia Inn, which offers rooms starting at $150 per night. More information can be found at www.seasideamelia.com or by calling +1 904-206-5300.

Peters Point Beachfront Park is another fantastic beach destination located at 4600 Peters Point Rd, Fernandina Beach. Known for its expansive sandy shores and easy vehicle access, this beach is popular among both locals and tourists. Visitors can drive directly onto the beach, making it a perfect spot for those with heavy beach gear or those who prefer tailgating by the ocean. The park offers free entry, with parking, restrooms, and picnic areas available. Those interested in staying nearby can check out The Ritz-Carlton, Amelia Island, where rooms start at $400 per night. Reservations and more information can be accessed at www.ritzcarlton.com or by calling +1 904-277-1100.

Kayaking, paddleboarding, and boating are popular activities on Amelia Island, given its rich network of waterways and scenic coastal views. Visitors can explore the island's beautiful marshes, creeks, and estuaries through guided tours or by renting equipment. Kayak Amelia, located at 13030 Heckscher Dr, Jacksonville, provides kayak and paddleboard rentals, with prices starting at $40 for a half-day rental. They also offer guided eco-tours that take visitors through the island's unique coastal ecosystems. More information is available at www.kayakamelia.com or by calling +1 904-251-0016. For those interested in a more luxurious boating experience, Windward Sailing offers private sailboat charters starting at $250 per tour. Their website is www.windwardsailing.com, and they can be reached at +1 904-327-3265.

Fishing and wildlife watching are other highlights of Amelia Island. Whether casting a line from the shore, booking a charter, or birdwatching in a nature reserve, visitors can experience a rich diversity of marine and avian life. Amelia Island Bait and Tackle, located at 1925 S 14th St, Fernandina Beach, offers fishing gear rentals and charters starting at $75 per trip. More details can be found at www.ameliaislandbaitandtackle.com or by calling +1 904-277-0775. Egan's Creek Greenway, a 300-acre nature preserve, is one of the best spots for wildlife observation. Visitors can see a variety of bird species, turtles, and even alligators in their natural habitat. Admission is free, and the preserve is open year-round.

Biking and hiking trails provide an excellent way to explore the island's landscapes. The Amelia Island Trail, stretching 6.2 miles, is a favorite among cyclists and pedestrians. The trail connects to the Timucuan Trail, offering an extended ride through Florida's coastal wilderness. Bikes can be rented from SuperCorsa Cycles at 4925 First Coast Hwy, Fernandina Beach, with rates starting at $25 per day. More information is available at www.supercorsacycles.com or by calling +1 904-310-9583. Another great hiking spot is Fort

Clinch State Park, where visitors can enjoy miles of scenic trails surrounded by diverse flora and fauna. Entry to the park is $6 per vehicle, and details can be found at www.floridastateparks.org/parks-and-trails/fort-clinch-state-park or by calling +1 904-277-7274.

Chapter 4

Where to Stay – Hotels, Resorts & Vacation Rentals

Luxury resorts and boutique hotels offer an indulgent experience, featuring upscale amenities, fine dining, and breathtaking ocean views. The Ritz-Carlton Amelia Island is one of the most prestigious options, known for its exceptional service and world-class facilities. Located at 4750 Amelia Island Pkwy, this resort boasts spacious rooms with elegant decor, a luxurious spa, and an 18-hole championship golf course. Guests can indulge in gourmet dining at Salt, a renowned on-site restaurant. The cost of staying at The Ritz-Carlton varies based on the season and room type, typically starting at $600 per night. Contact details include phone number (904) 277-1100 and website www.ritzcarlton.com

Another upscale option is the Omni Amelia Island Resort, situated at 39 Beach Lagoon Road. This oceanfront property features a full-service spa, multiple pools, and a variety of dining options. The resort caters to both families and couples, offering recreational activities such as kayaking, tennis, and biking. Room rates begin at approximately $400 per night. Reservations can be made by calling (904) 261-6161 or visiting www.omnihotels.com

For those looking for a charming boutique hotel experience, the Elizabeth Pointe Lodge is a great choice. Located at 98 S Fletcher Ave, this beachfront inn provides a peaceful and intimate atmosphere. Guests enjoy complimentary breakfast, evening wine and hors d'oeuvres, and personalized service. The cost per night typically starts at $300. For more information, call (904) 277-4851 or visit www.elizabethpointelodge.com

Budget-conscious travelers will find several affordable lodging options that offer comfort and convenience without a high price tag. Hampton Inn & Suites Amelia Island, located at 19 S 2nd St, is a popular choice for its central location near Historic Downtown Fernandina Beach. The hotel provides complimentary breakfast, free

Wi-Fi, and a fitness center. Prices start at around $180 per night. To book a stay, call (904) 491-4911 or visit www.hilton.com

Another budget-friendly option is the Seaside Amelia Inn at 2900 Atlantic Ave. This charming hotel offers direct beach access, complimentary breakfast, and cozy rooms. Room rates start at approximately $160 per night. For reservations, call (904) 206-5300 or visit www.seasideamelia.com

For travelers who prefer a more private and home-like experience, vacation rentals provide an excellent alternative. Oceanfront properties offer stunning views and direct access to the beach. Amelia Island Vacation Rentals features a range of accommodations, from cozy beach cottages to luxury condominiums. Rentals vary in price, with one-bedroom condos starting at $150 per night and larger beachfront homes reaching $500 or more per night. Booking and inquiries can be made through www.ameliaislandvacations.com

Another reputable vacation rental service is Stay Better Vacations, which offers a curated selection of properties across the island. Whether looking for a romantic retreat or a spacious home for a family gathering, visitors can find suitable options. Prices depend on location, size, and season, with contact details available at www.staybettervacations.com

For those traveling with an RV or seeking a camping experience, Amelia Island has excellent options. Fort Clinch State Park, located at 2601 Atlantic Ave, offers a scenic camping area with direct beach access, hiking trails, and historic sites. Campsites accommodate both tents and RVs, with amenities including restrooms, showers, and picnic areas. The cost for camping is around $26 per night. Reservations can be made through www.floridastateparks.org or by calling (904) 277-7274.

Another camping option is Amelia Island RV Resort, which caters specifically to RV travelers. Situated at 600 S 8th St, this resort provides full hook-up sites, a clubhouse, and recreational facilities. Rates start at $55 per night, with long-term stay discounts available. To book a

spot, call (904) 225-5577 or visit
www.ameliaislandrvresort.com

Chapter 5

Where to Eat

The seafood offerings on Amelia Island are among the best in Florida. One of the most popular spots is Timoti's Seafood Shak, known for its casual atmosphere and fresh, locally sourced seafood. The menu includes shrimp baskets, blackened fish tacos, and delicious clam chowder. The average meal cost ranges from $10 to $20 per person. It is located at 21 N 3rd St, Fernandina Beach, FL 32034. Contact them at (904) 310-6550 or visit their website at www.timotis.com

For an upscale seafood dining experience, Salt at The Ritz-Carlton is an excellent choice. This award-winning restaurant offers expertly crafted seafood dishes such as butter-poached lobster and sea scallops with truffle risotto. The ambiance is elegant, making it ideal for a romantic evening or a special occasion. Prices range from $50 to $100 per person. Salt is located at 4750 Amelia Island Pkwy, Fernandina Beach, FL 32034. Reservations can be made by calling (904) 277-1100 or visiting www.ritzcarlton.com

Southern cuisine is an integral part of Amelia Island's food culture. The Beach Diner is a popular spot for a hearty Southern-style breakfast or brunch. Guests can enjoy classic dishes like shrimp and grits, biscuits and gravy, and homemade corned beef hash. Prices typically range from $8 to $15 per person. The Beach Diner is located at 2006 S 8th St, Fernandina Beach, FL 32034. For more information, call (904) 310-3750 or visit www.beachdineramelia.com

Another must-visit Southern eatery is Shuckers, which is famous for its fried shrimp, hush puppies, and flavorful crab cakes. This restaurant provides a laid-back setting with excellent customer service. Meals cost between $15 and $30 per person. Shuckers is located at 96098 Victoria's Place, Yulee, FL 32097. They can be reached at (904) 849-0690, and their website is www.shuckersamelia.com

For those who enjoy waterfront dining, Brett's Waterway Cafe is a fantastic choice. Located on the marina, this restaurant offers stunning views of the Amelia River while serving dishes like blackened redfish and filet mignon. Prices range from $25 to $50 per person. The address is 1 Front St, Fernandina Beach, FL 32034. Call (904) 261-2660 or visit www.brettswaterwaycafe.com for reservations.

Another great waterfront restaurant is The Sandbar & Kitchen. Located directly on the beach, it offers a vibrant atmosphere with live music and an extensive menu that includes fresh oysters, lobster rolls, and craft cocktails. Expect to pay around $15 to $40 per person. It is located at 2910 Atlantic Ave, Fernandina Beach, FL

32034. For details, call (904) 310-3648 or visit
www.thesandbarandkitchen.com

Amelia Island also boasts excellent coffee shops, bakeries, and ice cream parlors. Amelia Island Coffee is a beloved café offering freshly brewed coffee, homemade pastries, and a cozy ambiance. It is an ideal place for a morning pick-me-up or a relaxing afternoon. Prices range from $3 to $10. The café is located at 207 Centre St, Fernandina Beach, FL 32034. Contact them at (904) 321-2111 or visit www.ameliaislandcoffee.com

For those with a sweet tooth, Nana Teresa's Bake Shop is a must-visit. This charming bakery offers delectable treats like cinnamon rolls, cupcakes, and handcrafted macarons. Prices are typically between $2 and $8 per item. The bake shop is located at 13 N 3rd St, Fernandina Beach, FL 32034. They can be reached at (904) 277-7977, and their website is www.nanateresasbakeshop.com

For ice cream lovers, Fernandina's Fantastic Fudge is a classic stop. In addition to their famous homemade fudge, they offer a variety of ice cream flavors made with high-quality ingredients. Ice cream cones and sundaes cost between $4 and $8. The shop is located at 218 Centre St, Fernandina Beach, FL 32034. For more information, call (904) 277-4801 or visit www.fantasticfudge.com

Those looking for a lively nightlife scene will find plenty of options in Amelia Island. The Palace Saloon, Florida's oldest continuously operating bar, is a must-visit destination. This historic establishment serves expertly crafted cocktails and has a lively atmosphere with live music on select nights. Drinks range from $5 to $15. It is located at 117 Centre St, Fernandina Beach, FL 32034. For inquiries, call (904) 491-3332 or visit www.thepalacesaloon.com

For craft beer enthusiasts, Mocama Beer Company is an excellent brewery featuring a wide selection of locally brewed beers. The spacious taproom and outdoor seating make it a great place to relax with friends. Beers typically cost between $6 and $10 per pint. Mocama Beer Company is located at 629 S 8th St, Fernandina

Beach, FL 32034. They can be contacted at (904) 310-9243, and their website is www.mocama.com

Another great bar option is The Decantery, a sophisticated wine and cocktail lounge offering an extensive selection of wines, handcrafted cocktails, and delicious small plates. Drinks cost between $8 and $20. The lounge is located at 117 Centre St, Fernandina Beach, FL 32034. For reservations and more information, call (904) 580-1230 or visit www.thedecantery.com

Chapter 6

Shopping & Local Markets

Boutique shops in Downtown Fernandina Beach are some of the most visited retail destinations on Amelia Island. These locally owned stores offer everything from stylish clothing and accessories to coastal home decor. Twisted Sisters! is a favorite among visitors, providing a selection of trendy women's fashion, jewelry, and home decor with a coastal flair. The cost of items varies, with clothing ranging from $30 to $100 and accessories starting at $15. It is located at 402 Centre Street, and visitors can call (904) 261-2501 or visit www.twistedsistersamelia.com for more details.

For those interested in fine clothing and gifts, Pearl Boutique offers an elegant selection of women's fashion and accessories. The boutique carries luxury brands, and shoppers can expect to find apparel ranging from $50 to $200. The store is located at 503 Centre Street, with contact available at (904) 277-2646 and online at www.pearlboutiqueamelia.com. Nearby, The Plantation Shop specializes in furniture, home accessories, and European antiques. It is located at 4828 First Coast Highway, with an estimated price range of $50 to $1,500 for unique home items. More information can be found at www.plantationshop.com or by calling (904) 261-2030.

Art enthusiasts can explore local galleries that showcase handcrafted souvenirs and artwork by regional artists. The Amelia SanJon Gallery is a must-visit for those looking for one-of-a-kind paintings, pottery, and sculptures. The gallery features works from renowned local artists and has price ranges from $50 to $2,000 depending on the art piece. It is located at 218 Ash Street and can be contacted at (904) 491-8040 or through www.ameliasanjongallery.com

Blue Door Artists is another destination for those interested in unique, handcrafted art pieces. This collective of local artists offers a variety of works, including paintings, jewelry, and mixed media art. Prices vary, but smaller pieces start at $25, with larger artworks priced upwards of $500. The gallery is located at 205 Centre Street, and more details can be found at www.bluedoorartists.com or by calling (904) 491-7733.

Visitors who enjoy fresh, locally sourced food will appreciate the farmers markets on Amelia Island. The Fernandina Beach Market Place is a weekly event held every Saturday from 9:00 AM to 1:00 PM in the historic downtown area. This market features fresh fruits, vegetables, baked goods, local honey, and handcrafted products from local artisans. Prices vary depending on vendors, but shoppers can expect to pay around $5 for fresh produce and $10-$20 for specialty food items. It is located at 25 N. 7th Street, and more details are available at www.fernandinabeachmarketplace.com or by calling (904) 557-8229.

Another excellent option is the Amelia Island Market, held on select Sundays at The Shops of Amelia Island Plantation. This market offers organic produce, handmade crafts, and fresh seafood. Costs vary, but shoppers typically find seafood priced at $10 per pound and handmade goods ranging from $15 to $50. More information is available at www.ameliaislandmarket.com, and the market can be reached at (904) 432-7086.

For those who love antiquing and discovering rare finds, Amelia Island has several antique shops that offer vintage treasures. Eight Flags Antique Market is one of the most well-known establishments, offering a variety of antiques, collectibles, and rare furniture pieces. Prices range widely, with small collectibles starting at $10 and larger furniture pieces going up to $2,000. It is located at 602 Centre Street, and visitors can call (904) 277-8550 or check www.eightflagsantiques.com for more details.

Trailer Park Collectibles is another destination for unique finds. This eclectic shop features a mix of vintage items, home decor, and local artwork. Prices range from $5 for small trinkets to over $500 for larger antique pieces. The store is located at 213 Beech Street, and more details can be found at www.trailerparkcollectibles.com or by calling (904) 310-9196.

For visitors who plan on staying near these shopping destinations, several hotels and resorts offer convenient accommodations. The Ritz-Carlton, Amelia Island is a luxury beachfront resort located at 4750 Amelia Island Parkway, offering elegant accommodations with rooms starting at approximately $600 per night. It features a full-service spa, fine dining, and oceanfront views. Reservations can be made at www.ritzcarlton.com or by calling (904) 277-1100.

The Addison on Amelia is a charming bed and breakfast located in the historic district at 614 Ash Street. Rooms start at around $250 per night, and guests enjoy personalized service and gourmet breakfasts. More information is available at www.addisononamelia.com or by calling (904) 277-1604.

For a budget-friendly stay, the Hampton Inn & Suites Amelia Island is a great option, located at 19 South 2nd Street. Rooms start at approximately $180 per night, and the hotel provides comfortable accommodations within walking distance of shopping and dining. Reservations can be made at www.hamptoninnameliaisland.com or by calling (904) 491-4911.

Chapter 7

History & Culture of Amelia Island

Amelia Island holds a deep historical and cultural significance, shaped by centuries of diverse influences. This barrier island off Florida's northeast coast has been inhabited, fought over, and developed by various civilizations, leaving behind a rich legacy that continues to define its character.

The island's earliest known inhabitants were the Timucua people, a Native American group that lived in the region for thousands of years. They thrived in this coastal environment, relying on the abundant marine resources and fertile land. The Timucua were known for their complex societal structures, agricultural practices, and artistic expressions, including pottery and intricate shell carvings. European contact in the 16th century introduced significant changes to their way of life. Spanish explorers, led by Pedro Menéndez de Avilés, arrived in 1562, establishing a stronghold and bringing Catholic missionaries to convert the native population. The Timucua population declined due to disease and conflict, and by the 18th century, their presence had largely disappeared from the island.

Spanish rule on Amelia Island brought European architectural and cultural influences that remain evident today. The Spanish built fortifications and established settlements that contributed to the island's strategic importance. Over time, the island changed hands multiple times, with brief periods of control by the French, British, and even pirates.

The island's connection to piracy and smuggling has long fascinated historians and visitors alike. During the late 17th and early 18th centuries, the waters surrounding Amelia Island became a haven for notorious pirates, including Luis Aury and Jean Lafitte. The deep harbor and hidden inlets provided ideal conditions for smuggling goods, evading authorities, and launching raids on passing ships. Even after piracy was suppressed, Amelia Island's proximity to major trade routes made it a focal point for illicit activities, including the slave trade and rum running during Prohibition.

During the Victorian era, Amelia Island underwent significant transformation. The town of Fernandina Beach became a bustling port city, attracting merchants, shipbuilders, and wealthy families seeking coastal retreats. Elegant Victorian-style homes were constructed, many of which still stand today as preserved landmarks. The historic district, with its charming architecture and cobblestone streets, offers a glimpse into the grandeur of the 19th century. Visitors can walk through the area and admire structures such as the Fairbanks House, built in 1885, and the Nassau County Courthouse, which remains one of Florida's most well-preserved Victorian-era government buildings.

Amelia Island is home to several museums and cultural centers that showcase its storied past. The Amelia Island Museum of History, located in the historic jail building, provides an in-depth look at the island's evolution through exhibits, artifacts, and guided tours. It covers everything from Native American history to the Spanish, British, and American periods, as well as the impact of industries like shrimping and tourism. The museum frequently hosts events, educational programs, and walking tours that bring history to life.

Another notable institution is the Maritime Museum of Amelia Island, which delves into the island's seafaring heritage. Exhibits highlight shipwrecks, naval battles, and the lives of sailors who navigated the treacherous waters off the coast. Artifacts recovered from sunken ships offer tangible connections to the past, drawing history enthusiasts and researchers alike.

The island's African American history is preserved and celebrated at the American Beach Museum. Established to honor the legacy of American Beach, a historic African American resort community founded in the 1930s, the museum tells the story of resilience and cultural significance. During segregation, American Beach provided a safe and vibrant vacation destination for Black families, attracting prominent figures such as Zora Neale Hurston and A. Philip Randolph. The museum explores the community's contributions, struggles, and ongoing efforts to preserve its heritage.

Chapter 8

Festivals & Events in 2025

Isle of Eight Flags Shrimp Festival is one of the most anticipated annual events, celebrating Amelia Island's long-standing connection to the shrimping industry. This festival features a grand parade, a juried arts and crafts show, live music, and, of course, a variety of shrimp dishes prepared by local chefs. Visitors can enjoy maritime-themed activities, including a pirate invasion, fireworks, and a boat parade. Admission is free, but food and merchandise vendors have individual pricing. The festival takes place in downtown Fernandina Beach, providing an excellent opportunity to explore the island's historic district. For more details, visit www.shrimpfestival.com or call (904) 261-3248. Nearby accommodations include the Hampton Inn & Suites Amelia Island, with rates starting at $180 per night, located at 19 S 2nd St, Fernandina Beach, FL. More information can be found at www.hamptoninnameliaisland.com or by calling (904) 491-4911.

Amelia Concours d'Elegance is a world-renowned luxury car show held annually at The Ritz-Carlton, Amelia Island. The event showcases rare and historic automobiles, drawing car enthusiasts, collectors, and industry experts. Guests can admire meticulously restored vintage cars, participate in expert panel discussions, and witness live auctions. General admission costs range from $175 to $350, depending on ticket packages. The 2025 event is scheduled for March 6-9 at The Golf Club of Amelia Island. For further information, visit www.ameliaconcours.com or call (904) 636-0027. Nearby accommodations include The Ritz-Carlton, Amelia Island, where room rates start at $599 per night. The resort is located at 4750 Amelia Island Pkwy, and reservations can be made at www.ritzcarlton.com/ameliaisland or by calling (904) 277-1100.

Holiday and seasonal events bring a magical touch to Amelia Island, attracting visitors who want to experience festive cheer. The Dickens on Centre holiday festival transforms downtown Fernandina Beach into a Victorian-era Christmas village. Visitors can enjoy holiday markets, horse-drawn carriage rides, and theatrical performances, making it an ideal destination for families and history enthusiasts. Admission to Dickens on Centre is free, though food and souvenirs are available for purchase. The event takes place in December, with exact dates available at www.ameliaisland.com/Dickens-on-Centre or by calling (904) 277-0717. For nearby lodging, the Amelia Schoolhouse Inn offers rooms starting at $230 per night at 914 Atlantic Ave, Fernandina Beach, FL. Reservations can be made at www.ameliaschoolhouseinn.com or by calling (904) 310-6264.

Local music and arts festivals contribute to the island's vibrant cultural scene. The Amelia Island Chamber Music Festival features performances by world-class musicians in intimate settings, making it a must-attend event for classical music lovers. Ticket prices vary by performance, with some concerts offering free admission. The festival spans from January through May at various locations across Amelia Island. More details can be found at www.ameliachambermusic.org or by calling (904) 261-1779. Another notable event is the Amelia Island Jazz Festival, held every October, featuring live jazz performances in a variety of styles, from swing to contemporary. Tickets range from $45 to $125 per event, with packages available for multiple concerts. The event takes place at different venues across the island. For more information, visit www.ameliaislandjazzfestival.com or call (904) 504-4772. A convenient lodging option for festival attendees is the Seaside Amelia Inn, with rates starting at $210 per night. The hotel is located at 2900 Atlantic Ave, Fernandina Beach, FL, and bookings can be made at www.seasideamelia.com or by calling (904) 206-5300.

Chapter 9

Day Trips & Nearby Attractions

Cumberland Island National Seashore, located just across the St. Marys River in Georgia, is one of the most pristine and untouched barrier islands in the United States. This federally protected park is known for its wild horses, unspoiled beaches, and extensive maritime forests. Visitors can explore the island's trails, visit the ruins of the Carnegie family's Dungeness Mansion, and observe diverse wildlife, including armadillos, deer, and a variety of bird species. The island is accessible only by ferry from St. Marys, Georgia, and there are no cars allowed, making it an ideal escape for nature lovers.

The ferry departs from St. Marys and requires advance reservations due to limited seating. The cost for the ferry ride is approximately $40 per adult and $30 per child, with an additional $10 entrance fee for the National Park Service. Camping is available for those who wish to extend their stay, with fees starting at $9 per night for a primitive campsite. For more information, visit www.nps.gov/cuis or call (912) 882-4336. Nearby hotels include the Riverview Hotel (rates from $150 per night, www.riverviewhotelstmarys.com, (912) 882-3242) and Spencer House Inn Bed & Breakfast (rates from $180 per night, www.spencerhouseinn.com, (912) 882-1872).

For those interested in a mix of urban attractions and beachside relaxation, Jacksonville, Florida, is a perfect day trip destination. Located just 30 miles south of Amelia Island, Jacksonville is home to a vibrant arts scene, professional sports teams, and beautiful beaches. Visitors can explore the Cummer Museum of Art & Gardens, catch a Jacksonville Jaguars football game at TIAA Bank Field, or enjoy the lively Jacksonville Beach area. The city also offers shopping and dining in the Riverside and Avondale districts, known for their historic charm and boutique storefronts.

Admission prices vary by attraction. The Cummer Museum charges $15 for adults, with discounts for seniors and students. Jacksonville Jaguars tickets range from $50 to $200, depending on the game and seating location. Jacksonville Beach is free to access and features numerous oceanfront restaurants and shops. For further details, visit www.visitjacksonville.com or call (904) 798-9111. Accommodation options include the One Ocean Resort & Spa (rates from $250 per night, www.oneoceanresort.com, (904) 249-7402) and Omni Jacksonville Hotel (rates from $180 per night, www.omnihotels.com, (904) 355-6664).

St. Augustine, the oldest city in the United States, is approximately a two-hour drive from Amelia Island. This historic town is famous for its Spanish colonial architecture, cobblestone streets, and well-preserved landmarks. Key attractions include the Castillo de San Marcos, a 17th-century fortress overlooking Matanzas Bay, and the Lightner Museum, housed in the former Alcazar Hotel. Visitors can also explore St. George Street, a pedestrian-friendly area filled with shops, restaurants, and historic buildings.

The Castillo de San Marcos entrance fee is $15 for adults, and children under 16 enter free. The Lightner Museum has a $17 admission fee, with discounts for seniors and students. Trolley tours are available for approximately $30 per person and provide a convenient way to see the city's main sights. For more information, visit www.visitstaugustine.com or call (904) 829-1711. Nearby accommodations include Casa Monica Resort & Spa (rates from $280 per night, www.casamonica.com, (904) 827-1888) and St.

George Inn (rates from $210 per night, www.stgeorge-inn.com, (904) 827-5740).

Nature enthusiasts can visit the Okefenokee Swamp, one of the most unique ecosystems in the southeastern United States. Spanning across Georgia and Florida, this vast wetland is home to alligators, cypress trees, and diverse bird species. Visitors can explore the swamp via guided boat tours, paddle through the waterways in a canoe, or hike one of the many scenic trails. The Okefenokee National Wildlife Refuge, located near Folkston, Georgia, is one of the best access points for exploring this natural wonder.

Boat tours typically cost around $25 to $30 per person, while canoe rentals start at $35 per day.

There is a $5 entrance fee for the wildlife refuge. Guided night tours are also available for those interested in seeing the swamp's nocturnal wildlife. For more information, visit www.fws.gov/refuge/okefenokee or call (912) 496-7836. Nearby accommodations include the Western Motel Folkston (rates from $75 per night, www.westernmotelga.com, (912) 496-4711) and Okefenokee Pastimes Cabins & Campground (rates from $100 per night, www.okefenokee.com, (912) 496-4472).

Chapter 10

Travel Tips & Essential Information

Amelia Island is a remarkable destination that offers a blend of historical charm, natural beauty, and modern comforts. Understanding key travel tips and essential information can enhance your experience, ensuring a seamless and enjoyable trip.

Safety and Travel Tips

Amelia Island is known for being a safe and welcoming destination. However, general travel precautions should always be followed. When visiting beaches, pay attention to flag warnings indicating water conditions. Riptides can occur, so it is advisable to swim only in designated areas with lifeguards. Carrying sunscreen and staying hydrated is crucial due to Florida's strong sun exposure, particularly in summer months.

Visitors should always lock their vehicles and keep valuables out of sight when parking at tourist sites or beaches. Downtown Fernandina Beach is safe for walking, but like any tourist destination, be mindful of your surroundings in less crowded areas, especially at night. If renting a bicycle, always wear a helmet and follow local traffic laws. Amelia Island has bike-friendly paths, but cyclists should remain alert to vehicular traffic.

In case of emergencies, dial 911. The closest hospital is Baptist Medical Center Nassau, located at 1250 South 18th Street, Fernandina Beach, FL 32034. The contact number is (904) 321-3500. Pharmacies such as Walgreens and CVS are available throughout the island for medical needs.

Packing List for Every Season

Amelia Island experiences a mild climate throughout the year, but packing appropriately ensures comfort. For summer visits, lightweight and breathable clothing, sunglasses, a wide-brimmed hat, and sandals are recommended. A reusable water bottle is useful for staying hydrated during outdoor activities.

Fall and spring bring milder temperatures, making light jackets and comfortable walking shoes ideal. Evening temperatures can drop, so a sweater or light hoodie may be necessary. Winter is relatively mild, but a medium-weight jacket is advisable for cooler evenings, particularly from December to February.

Outdoor adventurers should pack comfortable hiking shoes, insect repellent, and a rain poncho if visiting during the rainy season from June to

September. Beachgoers will benefit from quick-dry towels, waterproof phone cases, and reef-safe sunscreen.

Local Etiquette and Island Life

Amelia Island prides itself on being a friendly and relaxed community. Locals appreciate courteous visitors who respect the island's natural beauty and historic sites. Casual beach attire is acceptable in most places, but some upscale restaurants may require resort-casual clothing. Tipping is customary in restaurants, bars, and for services such as taxis and tour guides, typically ranging from 15-20% of the bill.

Eco-conscious travel is highly encouraged. Visitors should dispose of trash properly, avoid disturbing wildlife, and use reusable water bottles and bags. Many shops and restaurants participate in sustainability efforts, so supporting businesses with eco-friendly practices is recommended.

Emergency Contacts and Visitor Information

For travelers needing assistance, the Amelia Island Visitor Center provides maps, brochures, and guidance on accommodations and attractions. It is located at 102 Centre Street, Fernandina Beach, FL 32034. The contact number is (904) 277-0717, and more information can be found at www.ameliaisland.com.

For non-emergency assistance, the Fernandina Beach Police Department can be reached at (904) 277-7342. Visitors requiring consular assistance should check with their country's embassy in Jacksonville or Miami.

10 Days Itinerary

Day 1: Arrival and Relaxation Check into your hotel or vacation rental and explore Downtown Fernandina Beach. Enjoy dinner at a waterfront restaurant and take a leisurely stroll through the historic district.

Day 2: Beach Exploration Spend the day at Main Beach Park or Peters Point Beachfront Park. Enjoy sunbathing, beachcombing, or trying out water sports such as paddleboarding.

Day 3: Historic Fort Clinch State Park Visit Fort Clinch State Park to explore its well-preserved Civil War-era fort and scenic hiking trails. The cost of entry is approximately $6 per vehicle. Afterward, stop by The Palace Saloon for a historic drink experience.

Day 4: American Beach and Kayaking Adventure Learn about the African American heritage of American Beach, then embark on a kayaking tour through the salt marshes. Local tour operators such as Amelia Island Kayak Excursions offer guided trips starting at $55 per person. More details can be found at www.ameliakayak.com

Day 5: Shopping and Local Markets Spend the day exploring boutique shops in Downtown Fernandina Beach. Visit the Fernandina Beach Market Place on Saturdays to find local produce, handmade crafts, and souvenirs.

Day 6: Day Trip to Cumberland Island Take a ferry from St. Marys, Georgia, to Cumberland Island National Seashore. The ferry ride costs $40 per adult round trip. Enjoy hiking trails and wild horse sightings. More details can be found at www.nps.gov/cuis

Day 7: Golf and Spa Retreat Golf enthusiasts can visit the Amelia River Golf Club, with rates starting at $89 per round. Afterward, unwind at the Omni Amelia Island Resort Spa, where massage treatments start at $150. Reservations can be made at www.omnihotels.com

Day 8: Amelia Concours d'Elegance or Shrimp Festival If visiting in March, attend the Amelia Concours d'Elegance luxury car show at The Ritz-Carlton. Tickets start at $150. In May, experience the Isle of Eight Flags Shrimp Festival, which features seafood vendors and live music. More details can be found at www.ameliaconcours.com and www.shrimpfestival.com

Day 9: Biking and Outdoor Adventure Rent bikes and explore Amelia Island's scenic trails, including the Egans Creek Greenway. Bike rentals start at $20 per day from local shops like Beach Rentals and More. Kayak or fish in the Amelia River for a relaxing day outdoors.

Day 10: Farewell and Departure Enjoy a final breakfast at a cozy café such as Amelia Island Coffee. Take one last stroll along the beach before heading to Jacksonville International Airport, which is an hour's drive away.

Conclusion

For those who seek adventure, Amelia Island provides numerous opportunities to engage in water sports, hiking, biking, and wildlife watching. The island's well-preserved nature, combined with its welcoming community, makes it an ideal retreat for solo travelers, couples, and families alike. Whether you are paddling through the salt marshes, fishing off the shore, or simply relaxing on the sandy beaches, you will find a sense of peace and connection to nature that is truly unique.

History enthusiasts will be fascinated by Amelia Island's past, from its Native American roots and

Spanish influences to its stories of pirates and Victorian-era developments. The historic downtown of Fernandina Beach is a treasure trove of preserved buildings, boutique shops, art galleries, and local markets, offering a charming glimpse into the island's vibrant culture.

Events and festivals bring Amelia Island to life throughout the year. Whether you are attending the Isle of Eight Flags Shrimp Festival, enjoying the elegance of the Amelia Concours d'Elegance, or participating in seasonal celebrations, the island's community spirit is evident in every gathering. These events provide an excellent opportunity to engage with locals, enjoy regional cuisine, and experience the unique traditions that make Amelia Island special.

Practical travel considerations, such as accommodations, dining, and transportation, have been carefully covered in this guide to ensure a smooth and enjoyable trip. Whether you prefer the luxury of beachfront resorts, the charm of boutique hotels, or the affordability of vacation rentals, Amelia Island offers accommodations that cater to all budgets and preferences. Dining options are just as diverse, with a focus on fresh seafood, Southern delicacies, and international flavors.

Nearby attractions, including day trips to Cumberland Island, Jacksonville, and St. Augustine, further enhance the travel experience. These excursions provide an opportunity to explore more of Florida's history, wildlife, and coastal beauty beyond Amelia Island.

As you plan your visit, remember to embrace the island's laid-back atmosphere and friendly culture. Take time to appreciate the slow-paced lifestyle, stunning sunsets, and warm hospitality that define Amelia Island. Whether it's your first visit or a return trip, this destination has a way of creating cherished memories that last a lifetime.

Thank you for choosing this guide as your travel companion. May your journey to Amelia Island be filled with unforgettable moments, new discoveries, and the kind of relaxation that only a place this special can provide. Safe travels, and enjoy every experience that awaits you on this beautiful island.

Bonus

Would You Rather Game Question

Vacation (25 Questions)

1. Would you rather visit a tropical island or a snowy mountain resort?

2. Would you rather go on a road trip or take a flight to your destination?

3. Would you rather explore a new country every year or revisit your favorite place?

4. Would you rather stay in a luxury hotel or a cozy cabin?

5. Would you rather go on a safari or a deep-sea diving adventure?

6. Would you rather ride in a hot air balloon or a helicopter over scenic landscapes?

7. Would you rather travel solo or with a group of friends?

8. Would you rather visit a theme park or a historical landmark?

9. Would you rather try a local delicacy or stick to familiar food while traveling?

10. Would you rather spend a week at a beach resort or hiking in the mountains?

11. Would you rather go on a guided tour or explore a city on your own?

12. Would you rather visit famous cities or remote villages?

13. Would you rather spend your vacation sightseeing or relaxing?

14. Would you rather take a cruise or go camping?

15. Would you rather visit a place with warm weather or cool weather?

16. Would you rather have an all-inclusive resort stay or a budget-friendly backpacking trip?

17. Would you rather visit an amusement park or a water park?

18. Would you rather go whale watching or swim with dolphins?

19. Would you rather explore an underwater hotel or a treehouse resort?

20. Would you rather visit a desert or a rainforest?

21. Would you rather travel by train across a country or sail along the coast?

22. Would you rather take a sunset cruise or a sunrise hike?

23. Would you rather spend a month in Europe or in Asia?

24. Would you rather live abroad for a year or take a three-month world tour?

25. Would you rather go on a spontaneous trip or plan every detail?

Holiday (25 Questions)

26. Would you rather celebrate Christmas in the snow or on a sunny beach?

27. Would you rather have fireworks on every holiday or live in a town with no fireworks at all?

28. Would you rather receive one big gift or multiple small gifts?

29. Would you rather spend New Year's Eve at home with family or at a big party?

30. Would you rather celebrate your birthday with a quiet dinner or a big celebration?

31. Would you rather have unlimited holiday treats or unlimited holiday movies?

32. Would you rather spend Thanksgiving at home or travel somewhere special?

33. Would you rather wear matching pajamas on Christmas or ugly sweaters?

34. Would you rather have a holiday with just your immediate family or your extended family?

35. Would you rather decorate your entire house for Christmas or keep it simple?

36. Would you rather have a holiday where you only eat desserts or only savory food?

37. Would you rather receive only handmade gifts or only store-bought gifts?

38. Would you rather celebrate your birthday twice a year or not at all?

39. Would you rather have Halloween with only costumes or only candy?

40. Would you rather never celebrate Valentine's Day or never celebrate Halloween?

41. Would you rather take a holiday photo in matching outfits or in silly costumes?

42. Would you rather visit Santa at the North Pole or the Easter Bunny's secret hideout?

43. Would you rather get to open one present early or wait until Christmas morning?

44. Would you rather have a New Year's Eve party with family or friends?

45. Would you rather go ice skating or sledding during the holidays?

46. Would you rather have unlimited hot chocolate or unlimited gingerbread cookies?

47. Would you rather always have a white Christmas or a warm Christmas?

48. Would you rather spend the holidays at home or on vacation?

49. Would you rather decorate a Christmas tree or bake holiday cookies?

50. Would you rather have Thanksgiving dinner twice a year or Christmas twice a year?

Relaxation (25 Questions)

51. Would you rather get a massage or take a bubble bath?

52. Would you rather relax on a hammock or on a cozy couch?

53. Would you rather listen to ocean waves or rain falling?

54. Would you rather have unlimited candles or unlimited cozy blankets?

55. Would you rather spend a weekend at a spa or at a quiet cabin?

56. Would you rather sleep in every day or take afternoon naps?

57. Would you rather have a peaceful garden or a private beach?

58. Would you rather spend a day reading or watching movies?

59. Would you rather take a slow morning or have an early productive start?

60. Would you rather do yoga by the sea or meditate in a forest?

61. Would you rather have breakfast in bed or a picnic in the park?

62. Would you rather have a quiet night in or a peaceful walk under the stars?

63. Would you rather live in a house with a lake view or a mountain view?

64. Would you rather have a cozy night by the fireplace or a warm beach sunset?

65. Would you rather have a relaxing massage or a foot spa?

66. Would you rather sleep under the stars or in a luxury hotel?

67. Would you rather drink herbal tea or fruit-infused water?

68. Would you rather listen to calming music or sit in silence?

69. Would you rather take a slow scenic drive or a fast sports car ride?

70. Would you rather relax in a hot tub or a sauna?

71. Would you rather have a comfortable recliner or a big bean bag chair?

72. Would you rather spend the day in comfy pajamas or stylish loungewear?

73. Would you rather live in a quiet countryside or a peaceful beach town?

74. Would you rather wake up to birds chirping or waves crashing?

75. Would you rather enjoy a long, quiet walk or a lazy day in bed?

Night Out (25 Questions)

76. Would you rather go to a concert or a theater show?

77. Would you rather have dinner at a fancy restaurant or a casual food truck?

78. Would you rather go to a karaoke night or a game night?

79. Would you rather go bowling or play laser tag?

80. Would you rather go on a sunset boat ride or a city rooftop dinner?

81. Would you rather spend the night dancing or watching the stars?

82. Would you rather have a bonfire on the beach or a picnic under the stars?

83. Would you rather take a scenic night drive or walk along the waterfront?

84. Would you rather go to a comedy club or a magic show?

85. Would you rather go to a glow-in-the-dark party or a masquerade ball?

86. Would you rather take a nighttime ghost tour or visit a mystery escape room?

87. Would you rather go on a city bus tour at night or a boat cruise?

88. Would you rather watch the sunset from a skyscraper or a mountain top?

89. Would you rather have a moonlit dinner on the beach or a candlelit rooftop dinner?

90. Would you rather visit a 24-hour diner or a late-night coffee shop?

91. Would you rather spend the night at an amusement park or a carnival?

92. Would you rather have a night out with just one friend or a big group?

93. Would you rather take a dance class or a cooking class for a night out?

94. Would you rather explore a hidden speakeasy or a trendy rooftop bar?

95. Would you rather visit a jazz club or a street music festival?

96. Would you rather go stargazing in the desert or watch city lights from a rooftop?

97. Would you rather have a surprise night out planned for you or plan it yourself?

98. Would you rather take a limo ride around town or a bike ride under the stars?

99. Would you rather go to a night market or a street food festival?

100. Would you rather end the night with ice cream or a warm drink?

Made in United States
Orlando, FL
13 May 2025

61248263R00069